ASHEVILLE

Meditative Coloring Book

Escape to the best of Asheville;
adult coloring for relaxation, meditation,
stress reduction, spiritual connection,
prayer, healing, and coming into your
deep, true self; ages 9 to 109

Aliyah Schick

Sacred
Imprints

www.MeditativeColoring.com

Books by Aliyah Schick

- Angels Meditative Coloring Book 1
- Crosses Meditative Coloring Book 2
- Ancient Symbols Meditative Coloring Book 3
- Hearts Meditative Coloring Book 4
- Labyrinths Meditative Coloring Book 5
- OM Meditative Coloring Book 6
- Goddess Meditative Coloring Book 7
- Be Love Meditative Coloring Book 8
- Asheville Meditative Coloring Book 9

- Judaica Jewish Coloring Book for Grown Ups
- Chai Jewish Coloring Book for Grown Ups
- Alefbet Jewish Coloring Book for Grown Ups
- Star of David Jewish Coloring Book for Grown Ups

- The Labyrinth Guided Journal, A Year in the Labyrinth
- Mary Magdalene's Words:
    Two Women's Spiritual Journey,
    Both Truth and Fiction, Both Ancient and Now
- The Mary Magdalene Book: Mary Magdalene Speaks,
    Her Story and Her Message
- Finally, a Book of Poetry by Aliyah Schick

Dedicated to
Asheville's unique,
inclusive, and quirky
personality, and
the glorious land,
mountains, and nature
that surround us.

Dance! © 2017 Aliyah Schick

Table of Contents

Meditative Coloring and Asheville

Come to Asheville in your daydreams as you color these 36 original artist's drawings. Whether you live in Asheville, North Carolina, vacation here, remember summer camp here as a kid, or maybe you have yet to arrive, let go of every day life, take some deep, releasing breaths, and relax into the area's many delights. Immerse yourself in Asheville's marvelous and varied charms -- old time fiddler, mountain scene, historic architecture, kayaker on the river, meditation, Blue Ridge Parkway, craft beer, yoga, every kind of music, dance, drumming, lifestyle, and faith. Ground yourself into these mystical, magical mountains and feed your soul with meditative coloring in Asheville's welcoming embrace.

MEDITATION   © 2017 Aliyah Schick

Asheville Introduction

Nestled into a beautiful river valley within the the Southern Appalachian Mountains' Blue Ridge is the enchanting small city of Asheville, North Carolina. Its rich architectural heritage, lively arts and music culture, flourishing food and beer offerings, and incomparable outdoor recreation is home to 85,000 diverse city residents and another 350,000 in the surrounding four county's mountains. A popular southern vacation and retreat destination for over a hundred years, Western North Carolina and the city of Asheville frequently show up in "Top Places" articles and welcome more than five million visitors throughout each year.

Asheville History

The Cherokee

All of Western North Carolina was homeland to the Cherokee people when the first Europeans arrived in the year 1540 with Spanish explorer Hernando de Soto. Colonization followed and then conflicts escalated, eventually leading to a focused effort to destroy the Cherokee. In 1838 the U.S. Army forced the entire remaining native population to move to Oklahoma in the tragic "Trail of Tears." Those Cherokee who managed to stay here, or came back, became today's Eastern Band of Cherokee while survivors of the devastating march west founded the Western Band.

The Cherokee Nation   © 2017 Aliyah Schick

Asheville

The new settlers officially established the village of Morristown in 1793 at the crossing of two Native American trails near the joining of the French Broad and Swannanoa Rivers. Morristown was renamed Asheville a few years later in honor of North Carolina Governor Samuel Ashe. Because of the rough terrain and lack of access, the whole area stayed remote and isolated well into the 1800's. In 1828 a single lane, two-track dirt road followed the French Broad River to open the way west into Tennessee.

Civil War

The Civil War didn't come directly into Asheville until its very end in 1865. By then the town's population was about 2,500. Small companies of Union soldiers tried to attack but withdrew several times, and then a retreating Union army came in, took control, plundered, and burned homes. Like in most of the South, life was hard in Western North Carolina during the years after the war.

Railroad Prosperity

The first railroad finally connected Asheville to the east in 1880, bringing new growth of industry and population, and the area became a resort destination for the world's wealthiest families. The early 1900's saw stunning architecture go up in and around the city. Factories, businesses, residents, and prosperity bloomed in the 1910s and 1920s, and Asheville grew to briefly become the third largest city in the state.

1929 Depression

The Great Depression hit hard. City and county debt had soared along with optimism and expansion through the 1920s. Then with the Depression eight of the nine local banks failed, the economy stagnated, and growth ceased. Recovery from the depression took most of the rest of the 20th century. Fortunately the lack of new investment and construction meant that most of downtown Asheville's older buildings were saved, preserving the city's unique style.

New Vitality

Efforts to revitalize downtown took many years, determined citizens, and courageous investors and entrepreneurs. Now Asheville is flourishing again. The city makes top lists of all kinds, every year drawing more visitors, arts and music, lovers of outdoor recreation, businesses, and expanding population.

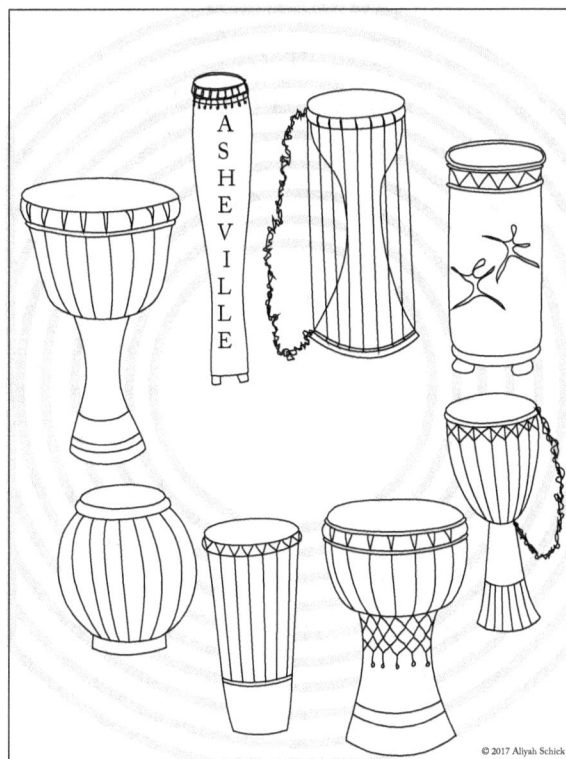

Drum Circle

© 2017 Aliyah Schick

Topographic Trail Map   © 2017 Aliyah Schick

Western North Carolina's Geology

About 300 million years ago, when continents were forming, moving, rifting apart, colliding, and then breaking apart again, the African continent rammed into the North American continent with such great impact that mountains taller than today's Himalayas were driven upward into a massive version of what we now call the Appalachian Mountains. Millions of years of erosion since then has worn away 90% of those original mountains and the Blue Ridge Mountains of Western North Carolina (WNC) are part of today's remnants. Imagine our mountains ten times as high as they are now. All of that has worn away by wind and rain.

The remaining rock, which used to be at the deepest layers, is a billion years old, making these mountains the oldest on earth. Having been subjected to extreme pressure and folding and fracturing and squeezing during all that geological turmoil, today's mountains are rich with gems and minerals, with quartz, mica, emeralds, aquamarines, rubies, sapphire, garnet, feldspar, and kaolin. There is evidence of people digging up precious materials in WNC for at least the past 2,000 years. The Spruce Pine Mining District, an hour's drive northeast of Asheville, has the world's best, purest supply of quartz, producing 90% of the quartz used in computers, cell phones, mp3 players, watches, solar panels, glass, ceramics, and lights. Mining provides the most jobs and money for several WNC counties.

Five of the ten highest peaks east of the Mississippi are in the section of the Blue Ridge called the Black Mountains, just east of Asheville. The tallest is Mount Mitchell at 6,684 feet, highest mountain east of the Mississippi River. The Roan Highlands and Great Craggies north of the Black Mountains also have a few tops above 6,000 feet.

The city of Asheville lies in the valley of the French Broad River between the Black Mountains to the east and the Great Smoky Mountains to the west, all part of the Southern Appalachian Mountains. The French Broad River flows north through Asheville, then west into Tennessee on its way to the Mississippi River.

The Great Smoky Mountains are named for the mist that rises off the heavy forests blanketing the highlands. The Smokies include several more of the region's highest peaks, large areas of federally protected wilderness and old-growth forest, and the Great Smoky Mountains National Park. Clingman's Dome is the highest peak in the Park at 6,643 feet.

The Great Balsam Mountains rise just east-southeast of the Great Smokies. Three significant rivers begin in the Balsams: the Pigeon, the French Broad, and the Tuckasegee. Two official wilderness areas, Shining Rock and Middle Prong, protect these valuable headwaters. Cold Mountain, 6,030 feet, known for the best selling book and movie of that name, is in the Shining Rock Wilderness area. The Blue Ridge Parkway follows the high ridges of the Balsams on its way from Asheville to the town of Cherokee and the entrance to Great Smoky Mountains National Park.

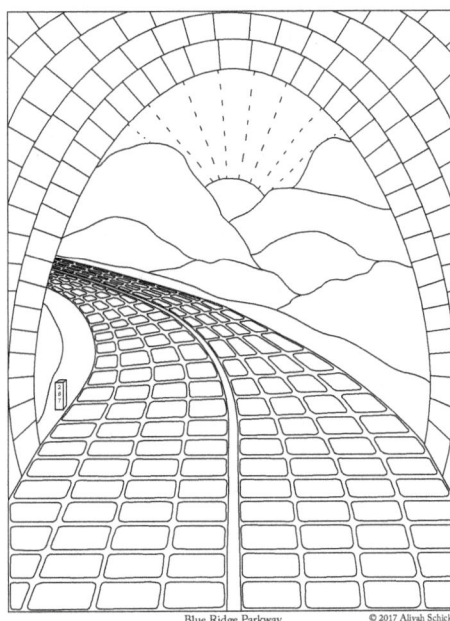

Blue Ridge Parkway   © 2017 Aliyah Schick

The Blue Ridge Parkway

The Blue Ridge Parkway starts at the Shenandoah National Park in Virginia and runs 469 miles southwest through Virginia and North Carolina to finally connect to the Great Smoky Mountains National Park in the far west of North Carolina. On its way the Parkway passes right through the Asheville area and across the Biltmore Estate. Construction of the Parkway began during President Franklin D. Roosevelt's administration and took 52 years to complete in 1987.

All along the 120 miles of Parkway in Western North Carolina there are hiking trails, waterfalls, swimming holes, many pull-out vistas, and several visitor centers.

Some highlights:

mile 304   Grandfather Mountain, Linn Cove Viaduct, visitor center, trails

mile 316.3   Linville Falls Recreation Area, Linville Falls, Linville Gorge, camping

mile 331   Museum of North Carolina Minerals

mile 355.4   Mount Mitchell State Park

mile 382   The Folk Art Center, Southern Highland Craft Guild, programs, galleries, library, book store

mile 382.6 to 393.6   Asheville exits

mile 384   The Blue Ridge Parkway Visitor Center, exhibits, theater, information

mile 408.6   Mount Pisgah, formerly part of the Biltmore Estate, Pisgah Inn Resort, campground, restaurant, gift shop

mile 420.2   Shining Rock Wilderness

mile 431   Richland Balsam, highest point on the Parkway at 6,053 feet above sea level

mile 451.2   Watercock Knob, panorama of the Great Smokies, visitor center, exhibits, trail

mile 469   Great Smoky Mountains National Park, Cherokee reservation, southern end of the Blue Ridge Parkway

The Great Smoky Mountains National Park

The Great Smoky Mountains National Park is about 50 miles west of Asheville, just over an hour's drive. It is the most visited national park in the U.S. with over 10 million visitors per year. The North Carolina park entrance is in Cherokee, NC, and just inside find the Oconaluftee Visitor Center with exhibits, history, information, maps, and souvenirs.

The Great Smoky Mountains are part of the Blue Ridge Mountains, which are part of the Appalachian Mountains. The park straddles the border between North Carolina and Tennessee following the ridge line of the mountains from northeast to southwest. One side of the park is in North Carolina and the other is in Tennessee.

The park's land, as well as most of Western North Carolina, was originally part of the Cherokee people's homeland. European settlers moved in beginning in the 1500s, and eventually in 1838 the Cherokee were forced out. A few managed to stay here by hiding in what is now the park, and others were able to return. Their descendants belong to the Eastern Band of the Cherokee. The Qualia Boundary, 56,000 acres next to the park on the North Carolina side, is home to 60% of their 13,000 enrolled members.

Sixteen mountains in the Great Smoky Mountains National Park are over 6,000 feet high, and the lowest point in the park is only 876 feet above sea level. This variation in elevation has created quite a range of ecological zones within the park. Plants and animals common to the northeast United States and Canada live at the park's higher elevations, and southern species live in the lower areas. As a result at least 10,000 species of plants and animals exist in the park.

Almost 95% of the land is forest, including over 100 species of trees, and almost 36% of that is old growth forest. Seventy miles of the Appalachian Trail runs right through the center of the park on the ridge line. There are nearly 800 miles of other trails to hike, and plenty of fishing, horseback riding, bicycling, and water tubing.

Popular Hiking Trails in WNC

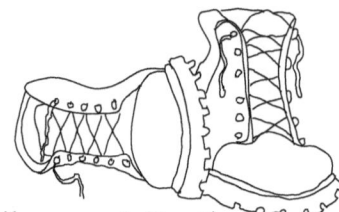

Asheville Urban Trail
Self-guided walking sculpture and history tour of downtown Asheville, easy, 1.7 miles.

Chimney Rock Park
Views of Lake Lure and Hickory Nut Gorge, trails easy to strenuous, 25 miles southeast of Asheville, admission fee.

Craggy Gardens
1.5 and 3 mile trails, moderate, great views, visitor center, rhododendron in bloom in June, on the Blue Ridge Parkway at milepost 364.4.

DuPont State Forest
Many trails and waterfalls, weekend crowds, visitor center, between Brevard and Hendersonville, 40-mile drive south from Asheville.

Gorges State Park
Waterfalls, river gorges, rain forest climate, rugged topography, visitor center, displays, some primitive campsites, located along the upper area of the Blue Ridge Escarpment, 53 miles south of Asheville between Brevard and Cashiers.

Grandfather Mountain
Nature preserve, many trails, easy to strenuous, great views, 70 miles north east from Asheville, just off the Blue Ridge Parkway on US 221.

Graveyard Fields
1 and 4 mile trails, moderate, two waterfalls, swimming hole, popular, on Blue Ridge Parkway at milepost 419.

Joyce Kilmer Memorial Forest
Easy 2 mile loop, old growth hardwood forest in the Nantahala National Forest, south of Great Smoky Mountains National Park, 2 hours from Asheville.

Lake Junaluska Walking Trail
Paved, accessible 2.3 mile loop around the lake at the United Methodist Conference and Retreat Center, open to the public. Labyrinth, footbridge across the dam, hotels, museum, welcome center. 25 miles west from Asheville.

Linville Falls
1.6 mile roundtrip trail, moderate, 4 overlooks, visitor center, nearby Linville Gorge and Linville Caverns, on Blue Ridge Parkway at milepost 316.

Looking Glass Rock
6.5 mile round trip trail, strenuous, climbs 1700 feet in just over three miles. Off US 276 in Pisgah National Forest, 36 miles southwest from Asheville.

Max Patch
Easy loop trails with great views, access to the Appalachian Trail, near Hot Springs, an hour drive northwest from Asheville.

Mount Mitchell
Multiple trails, one easy 3/4 mile loop, observation deck, small visitor center, on Blue Ridge Parkway at milepost 355.4.

Mount Pisgah
3 mile round trip hike to summit, strenuous, views from the top, on Blue Ridge Parkway at milepost 407.6.

North Carolina Arboretum
10 miles of trails, guided walks, special events, fee, call for information 828-665-2492, located just off NC 191 at entrance to the Blue Ridge Parkway in South Asheville.

Pink Beds
Easy woodland five-mile loop trail, wildflowers, on US 276 next to Cradle of Forestry in Pisgah National Forest, about one hour southwest from Asheville.

Skinny Dip Falls
1/2 mile moderate hike, waterfall and popular swimming hole, on Blue Ridge Parkway at milepost 417.

Sliding Rock
Very popular 60-foot long natural stone waterslide into an eight-foot deep pool, attracts thousands of visitors each summer. Fee when staff is on duty. Eight miles from Brevard on US 276 in the Pisgah National Forest, 42 miles from Asheville.

The Appalachian Trail

The Appalachian National Scenic Trail is a 2,200 mile foot trail that follows the high ridges of the Appalachian Mountains from the far north in Maine, and crosses New Hampshire, Vermont, Massachusetts, Connecticut, New York, New Jersey, Pennsylvania, Maryland, West Virginia, Virginia, Tennessee, North Carolina, and into northern Georgia. Thru-hikers walk the whole distance in one season. There are also lots of day hikers, weekend hikers, and section hikers. The AT follows the ridge crests of the southern portion of the Appalachian Mountains in Western North Carolina. There are many opportunities for short hikes on the Appalachian Trail near Asheville. For more information contact the Appalachian Trail Conservancy, www.appalachiantrail.org.

New Age in Asheville

Asheville always ranks high on any list of hippy towns. From downtown sidewalks to cooperative living groups to off-the-grid, back-mountain homesteads, both aging and youthful counter-culture creatives abound. Futon stores, long skirts and handmade sandals, vegan meals, yoga and meditation centers, street art and musical buskers, the purple LaZoom comedy tour bus, the French Broad Food Co-op, rock and crystal shops, alternative book stores, psychics and healers, Jubilee Community Church, demonstrations and rallies and prayer circles, feeding the hungry, moon and solstice celebrations, Earthaven Eco-Village, shamanic journeying, street people, candles and incense, and all kinds of self-transformation teachers and workshops all add up to a kaleidoscope of ways to drop out of at least some part of ordinary, starched-shirt living and into Asheville's paradoxical combination of mysticism and fun, weird and familiar, New Age and Bible Belt.

Sacred Geometry   © 2017 Aliyah Schick

The Asheville area is one of those places in the United States that those in the know identify as "high vibration," where the natural electromagnetic energy of the earth is extra strong and uplifting. A lot of Ashevilleans say they were undeniably drawn here. Some say there is a major energy vortex, or several, in Western North Carolina, creating a powerful energy flow that affects the whole area. As a matter of fact, 25% of the underlying rock in Western North Carolina is quartz.

Quartz

Quartz is a very pure, very high vibration crystalized mineral now used extensively in high tech applications such as computers, cell phones, mp3 players, watches and clocks, solar panels, and scientific equipment. Ninety percent of the highest quality quartz used worldwide comes from Spruce Pine, North Carolina, an hour northeast of Asheville.

The molecules of natural quartz crystal form hexagonal geometric patterns of precise latticework known to vibrate at very stable, coherent frequencies. Throughout all human existence natural quartz crystals have been used in sacred traditions by shamans, priests, and healers to tune, harmonize, increase, and project the energies of the body, mind, emotions, and spirit. Quartz is now widely used in science and technology to store, focus, amplify, and transmit energy and information. Our digital age lifestyle depends entirely on those exceptional qualities of quartz that were long ago recognized by the ancients.

Things to Do in the Asheville Area

Appalachian Trail, hiking

Asheville Art Museum, 20th century American art

Asheville Community Theater, since 1946; comedies, musicals, and dramas; outreach

Asheville Lyric Opera, professional opera

aSHEville Museum, women's museum; exhibits, gift shop, events, educational programs

Asheville Symphony Orchestra, professional 80-100 member orchestra

Asheville Urban Trail, 1.7 miles walking past 30 stations, downtown

Asheville Visitor Center, inside the Asheville Chamber of Commerce Building at 36 Montford Avenue; information, directions, maps, brochures, Wi-Fi, restrooms

Basilica of St. Lawrence, Roman Catholic, built in 1905, National Registry of Historic Places

Biltmore Estate, 19th century historic mansion and gardens, largest home in America, 8000-acre grounds, inn, winery, dining, shopping, events

Black Mountain College Museum and Arts Center, history, exhibits, workshops, events

Blue Ridge Parkway, 120 miles of the parkway crosses Western North Carolina's high country mountains; lodging, camping, hiking

Botanical Gardens of Asheville, native Southern Appalachian plants, trails, exhibits, programs

Brewery tours

Carl Sandburg Home National Historic Site, exhibits, farm, trails, historic buildings, in Flat Rock

Carrier Park, sports fields, courts, playground, picnic, trails, in West Asheville

Cataloochee Ski Area, Maggie Valley

Cathedral of All Souls, Episcopal, est. by George Vanderbilt II in 1896, Biltmore Village

Pack Square Park   © 2017 Aliyah Schick

Chimney Rock State Park, views, trails, rock climbing, gift shop

Diana Wortham Theater, 500 seat performing arts theater in downtown Asheville's Pack Square; nearby restaurants, museums, galleries

Drum Circle in Pritchard Park, downtown, Friday evenings spring through fall

Grandfather Mountain, views, trails, Mile-High Swinging Bridge, events, Nature Museum

Grove Arcade, shops, restaurants, offices, & apartments

Grove Park Inn, historic resort hotel, spa, golf, mountain views

Kayaking, canoeing, and tubing, quiet water to class IV and higher whitewater

LaZoom Comedy Bus Tours, award-winning, city tour, haunted tour, brewery tour, kids' tour

McCormick Field, oldest minor league baseball park in regular use; home of the Asheville Tourists, Single-A minor league baseball team affiliated with the Colorado Rockies; ball park in the 1988 movie Bull Durham

Montford Park Players, free summer "Shakespeare in the Park" put on by volunteer actors

North Carolina Arboretum, landscape, education, research, exhibits, events, membership

North Carolina Stage Company, professional theater, downtown

Pack Square Park, festivals, concerts, events, pavilion, 6.5 acres in the center of downtown

River Arts District, working artists' studios, galleries, restaurants

Riverside Cemetery, late 19th Century, Thomas Wolfe and O'Henry graves

Smith-McDowell House Museum, Asheville's oldest house, history, exhibits, Civil War Memorial

Southern Highlands Craft Guild Folk Art Center, network of 900 artists and mountain craftspeople, galleries, library & gift shop on the Blue Ridge Parkway

Thomas Wolfe House Memorial, boarding house Wolfe wrote about in Look Homeward, Angel, exhibits, tours, programs

YMI Cultural Center, established 1893, serving African-American culture, exhibits, events

Architectural Attractions

Asheville City Hall, Art Deco, 70 Court Plaza, downtown

Jackson Building, Neo-Gothic, 22 N. Pack Square, downtown

Grove Arcade, Neo-Tudor with Gothic details, 1 Page Avenue, downtown

The Basilica   © 2017 Aliyah Schick

Basilica of St. Lawrence, Spanish Baroque Revival, 97 Haywood Street, downtown

Grove Park Inn, Arts and Crafts Movement, 290 Macon Avenue, north of downtown

Biltmore House, French Renaissance, 1 Lodge Street, South Asheville

Biltmore Village, English manorial village, outside the entrance to Biltmore Estate

Cathedral of All Souls Episcopal Church and Parish Hall, Romanesque Revival, Biltmore Village

Montford Area Historic District, Victorian, Queen Anne, Arts & Crafts, and more, north of downtown, off Montford Avenue

Albemarle Park Historic District, Neoclassical, Tudoresque, Colonial Revival, Queen Anne, north of downtown, off Charlotte Street

Asheville Information Sources

Explore Asheville

    Asheville's Official Travel Site

    https://www.exploreasheville.com/

Asheville Visitor Center

    Information, directions, public restrooms, maps, brochures, Wi-Fi

    Purchase tickets for Biltmore, trolley tours, golf coupon books, help with lodging

    Downtown, 36 Montford Avenue, Asheville NC 28801

    (828) 258-6101

RomanticAsheville.com

    Insider's Guide to the NC Mountains

    Lodging, food & drink, Parkway, Biltmore, weddings, events, trip planner

ashvegas.com

    Independent news blog serving Asheville

    Local news, word on the street, events, information as it happens

    Follow on Facebook, Twitter, and Instagram for the latest news

WLOS.com/news/local

    Asheville local news, weather, sports

    Channel 13 TV

Citizen-Times

    Daily newspaper

    Local news, sports, entertainment

    www.citizen-times.com/local/

Mountain Xpress

    Weekly newspaper

    Independent news, arts, events

    Asheville and Western North Carolina

WCQS 88.1 FM Radio

    Listener supported public radio, local coverage, NPR news and programming, classical music, jazz, listen online

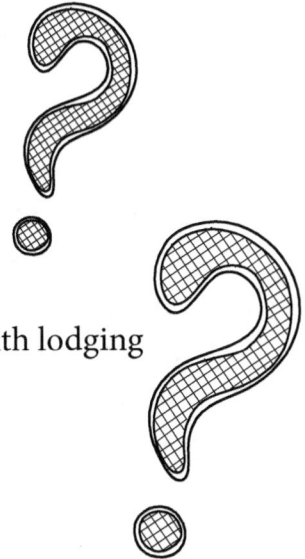

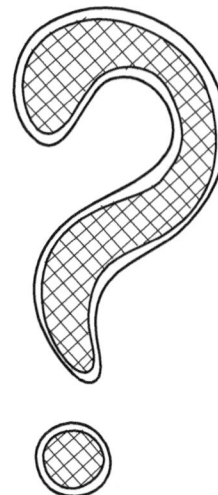

Suggestions for How to Use This Book

Use this *Asheville Meditative Coloring Book* to immerse yourself in the magical, mystical enchantment of Asheville. Come into your deep, true, spiritually attuned, mountain-seeking soul self. You may wish to experience coloring the images in quiet contemplation. Or, focus on a chant or affirmation or prayer as you work with colors. Or, ask for release and understanding regarding an issue you are dealing with. Or, ask for a clearer sense of some aspect of yourself and how it serves you. You may wish to learn more about your path or purpose in this lifetime.

Open your heart and your mind. Pay attention to impressions and ideas, feelings, intuition, and messages. They may very well be exactly what you need to hear.

Tools
Choose your favorite coloring tools, or you might like to gather a variety of pens, crayons, colored pencils, chalk, oil pastels, markers, glitter pens, paints, etc. You may want to place a blank sheet of paper behind the page so ink or paint does not go through.

Music
Consider playing a recording of soft instrumental background music.

Silence
You may prefer quiet, so that all your attention focuses inwardly and on what you are doing. Emptiness can give rise to profound experience.

Nature
A favorite spot outdoors can provide just the right environment for connecting with your deep self. Beach, woods, backyard, porch, treehouse, mountain top, woods, stream, pond, park, etc.

Meditation
You may like to meditate first, and then begin working with the colors. Try any of the many ways of meditation, or simply be with your breath for a few minutes, following it in and out. Or, you may wish to try the guided meditation on the next page. Read it silently or out loud, slowly, pausing to draw in each breath.

Guided Meditation for Coloring

Take in a breath... and on the exhale release the day's happenings, settling into this peaceful time of creative, spiritual connection.

Take in a breath... and on the exhale let go of worries and troubles and burdens. You can pick them up again later if you need to.

Take in a breath... and on the exhale come into the center of your self. From there drop a line down through your body, through the chair and the floor and into the earth. Continuing to breathe, drop down through soil and sand and stone, through coal and underground stream, and minerals and precious metals. Down through all the colors and textures and densities of the earth, down to the very center of the earth, to the heart of the mother. Tie your line there. Anchor yourself there.

Take in a breath... and on the exhale extend your line up from your center, through your body and out the crown of your head, up through the ceiling, the roof, and into the sky. Past clouds and wind and thinning gases, out through the atmosphere and into space. Past the sun and galaxy and stars and universe, out to the depths of the Source of All That Is. Feel your connection there. You are part of the great cosmos. You are one with all being.

Take in a breath... and on the exhale return to the drawing before you and ask that you be open to receiving guidance and understanding as you spend time with it. Know that there are no mistakes, only new choices and combinations and patterns that suggest new perception at an other-than-conscious level. Or that remind us of something that can now be released. Or that create an opening to new possibilities.

Take in a breath... and on the exhale release "shoulds" and rules and expectations. Let go and open to this new moment.

Now, begin by picking up whatever color catches your attention.

About the Artist/Author

Aliyah Schick has been an artist all her life. After Peace Corps in the Andes of South America, she worked in clay making pottery and ceramic art pieces, then in fibers and fabrics to make soft-sculptural wall pieces and art quilts and dolls designed to carry healing energy. Now she explores drawing, digital art, poetry, and prose. Aliyah's *Meditative Coloring Books* were among the earliest for grown ups, and continue to be popular because each one is so much more than just a coloring book.

At the heart of all this art, Aliyah's deep calling is healing. She is a skilled and dynamic Energy Medicine practitioner. Her work in the multidimensional layers and patterns of the auric field is well known, powerful, and effective. Her art, writings, and *Meditative Coloring Books* all rise up as new expressions of Aliyah's healing work. Entering into these drawings attracts that healing as it opens the way to remember who you really are, what matters, and why you are here.

Aliyah lives and works in the beautiful Blue Ridge Mountains of North Carolina, where the energy of the earth is easily accessible, ancient, motherly, and obvious. A place where people speak with familiarity and reverence of the land and spirit, and where the sacred comes to sit with us on the porch to share the afternoon sun.

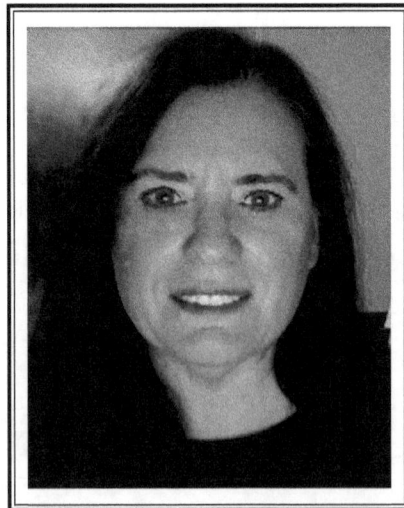

www.AliyahSchick.com

The Asheville Drawings

Opposite each Asheville drawing is an open space labeled Meditative Impressions. Use this space to catch and keep hold of your thoughts, wishes, intentions, affirmations, prayers, poems, memories, notes, drawings, or whatever comes to you as you explore coloring with this book.

Make it yours.

Asheville

Western North Carolina

23

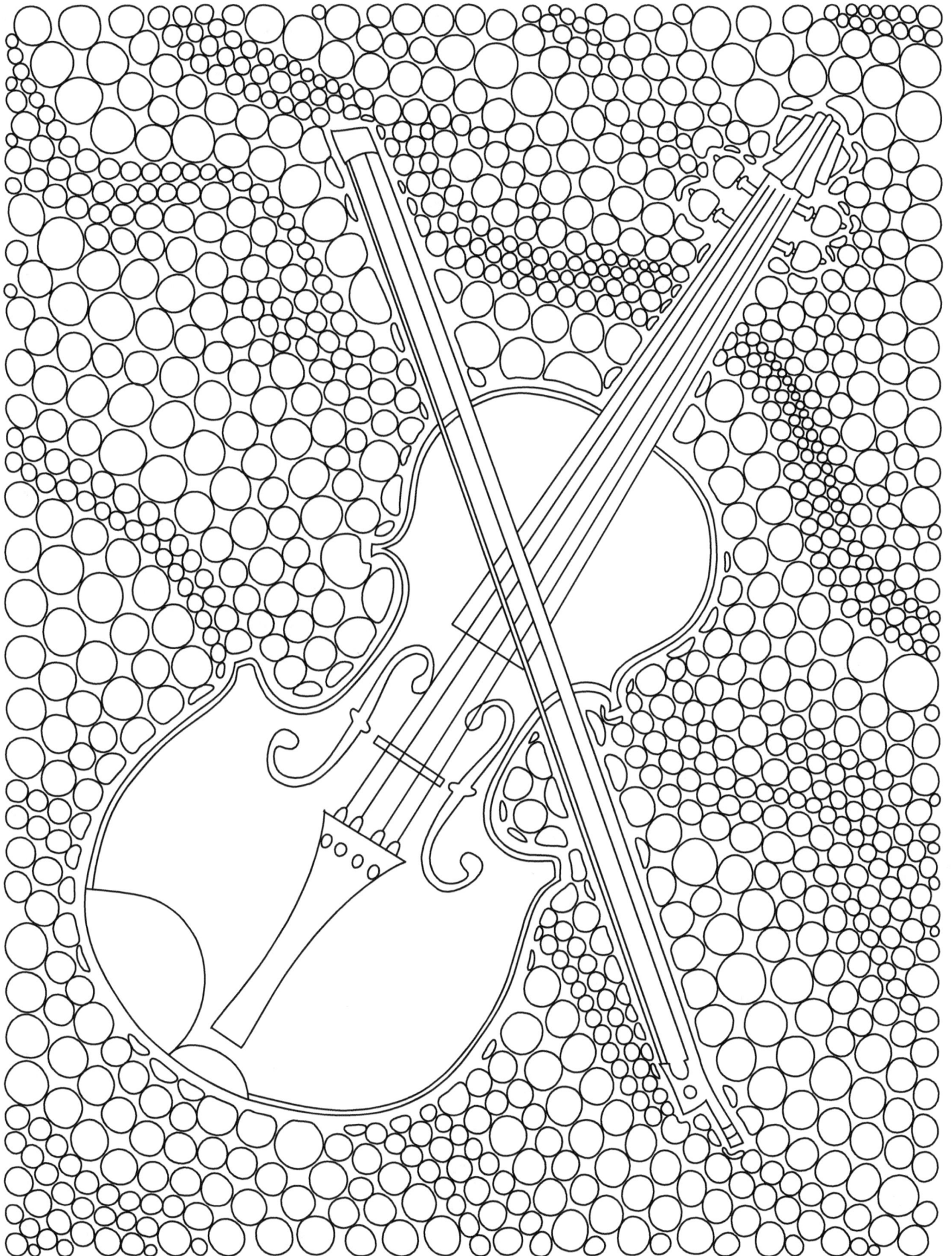

Asheville Symphony

© 2017 Aliyah Schick

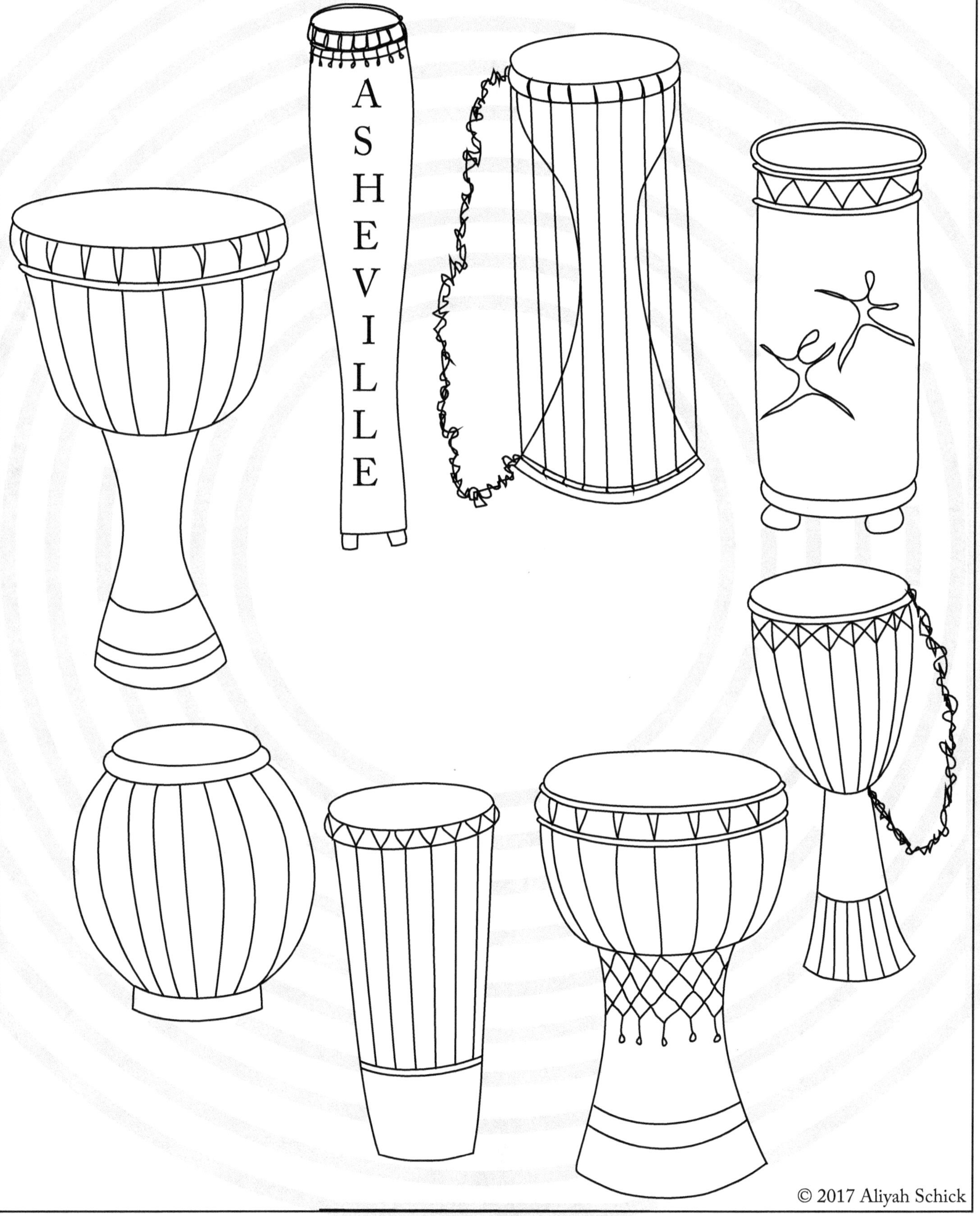

Pritchard Park Drum Circle

USA Best Asheville Beer North Carolina
COLD
Mountain
Beer
THE
A'VILLE
PUB
NEW WAY
BREWERY'S
APRIL
IPA

Local Breweries

© 2017 Aliyah Schick

Quartz Crystals

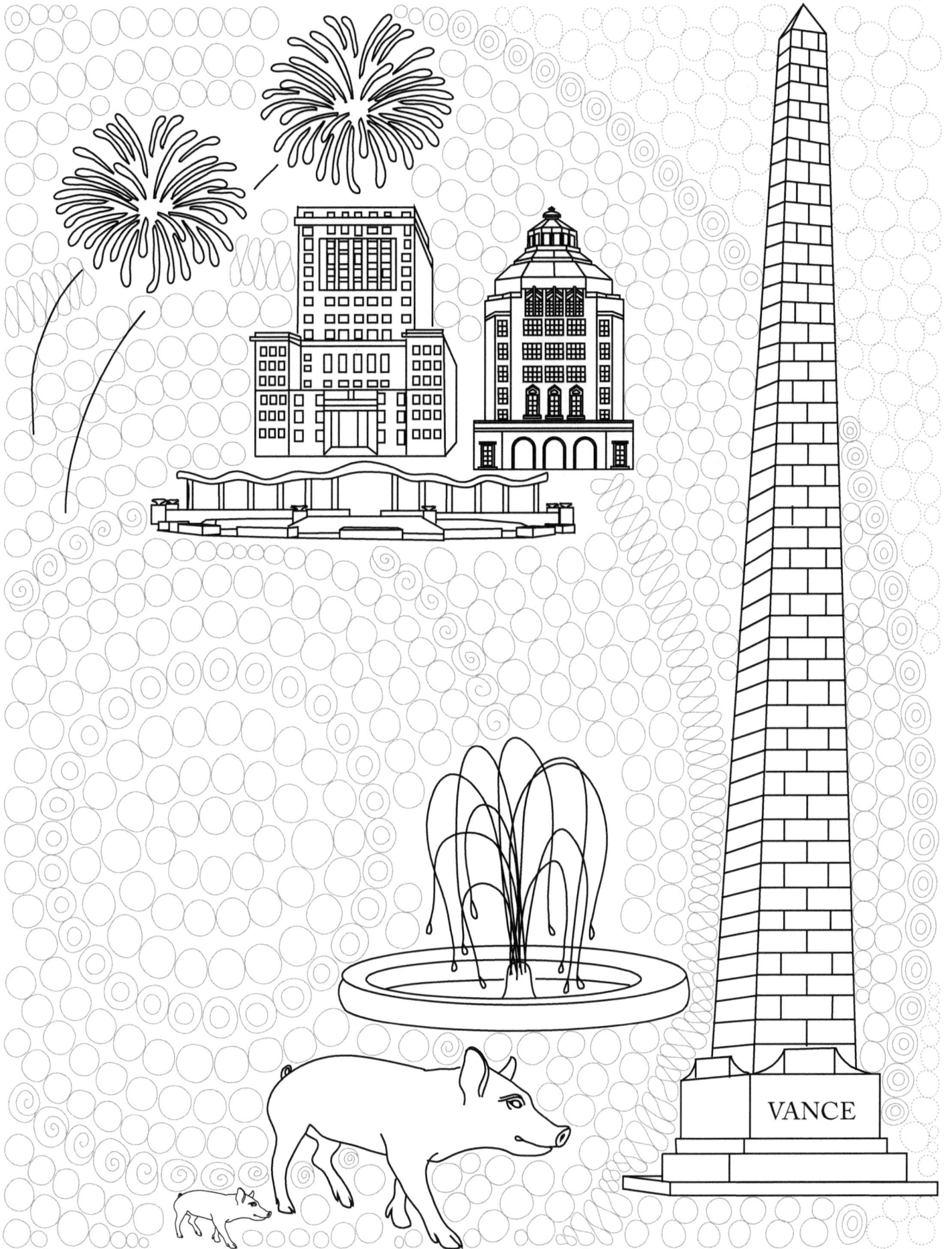

Pack Square Park

VANCE

33

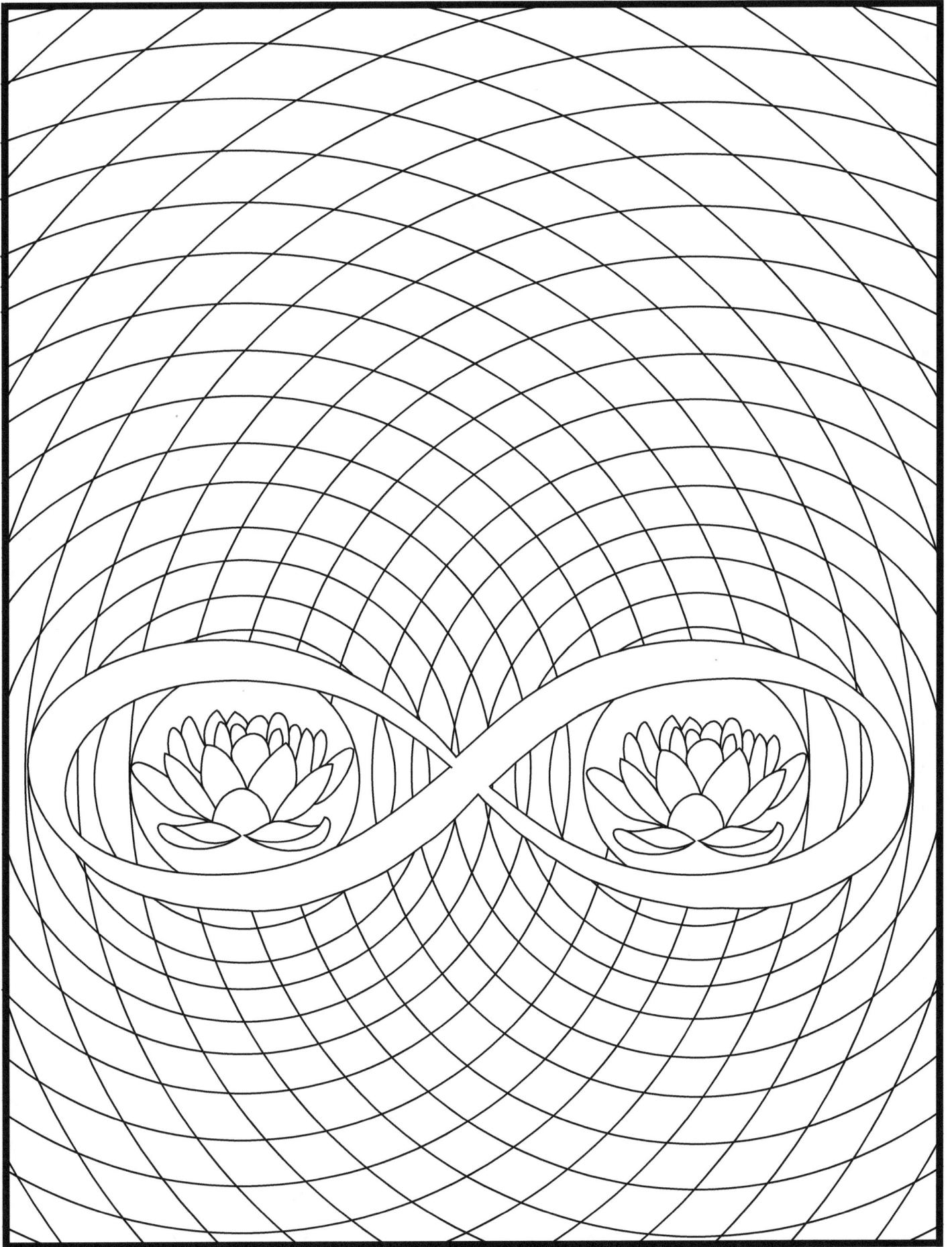

Infinite Possibilities

© 2017 Aliyah Schick

Yoga

The Blue Ridge Parkway

Lotus

41

A destiny that leads the English to the Dutch is strange enough; but one that leads from Epsom into Pennsylvania, and thence into the hills that shut in Altamont over the proud coral cry of the cock, and the soft stone smile of an angel, is touched by that dark miracle of chance which makes new magic in a dusty world.

Thomas Wolfe
Look Homeward, Angel
Asheville, 1929

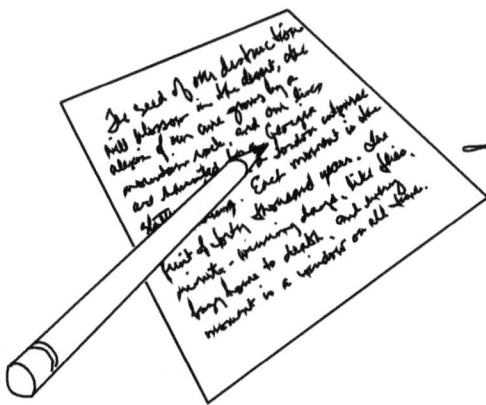

Thomas Wolfe Memorial

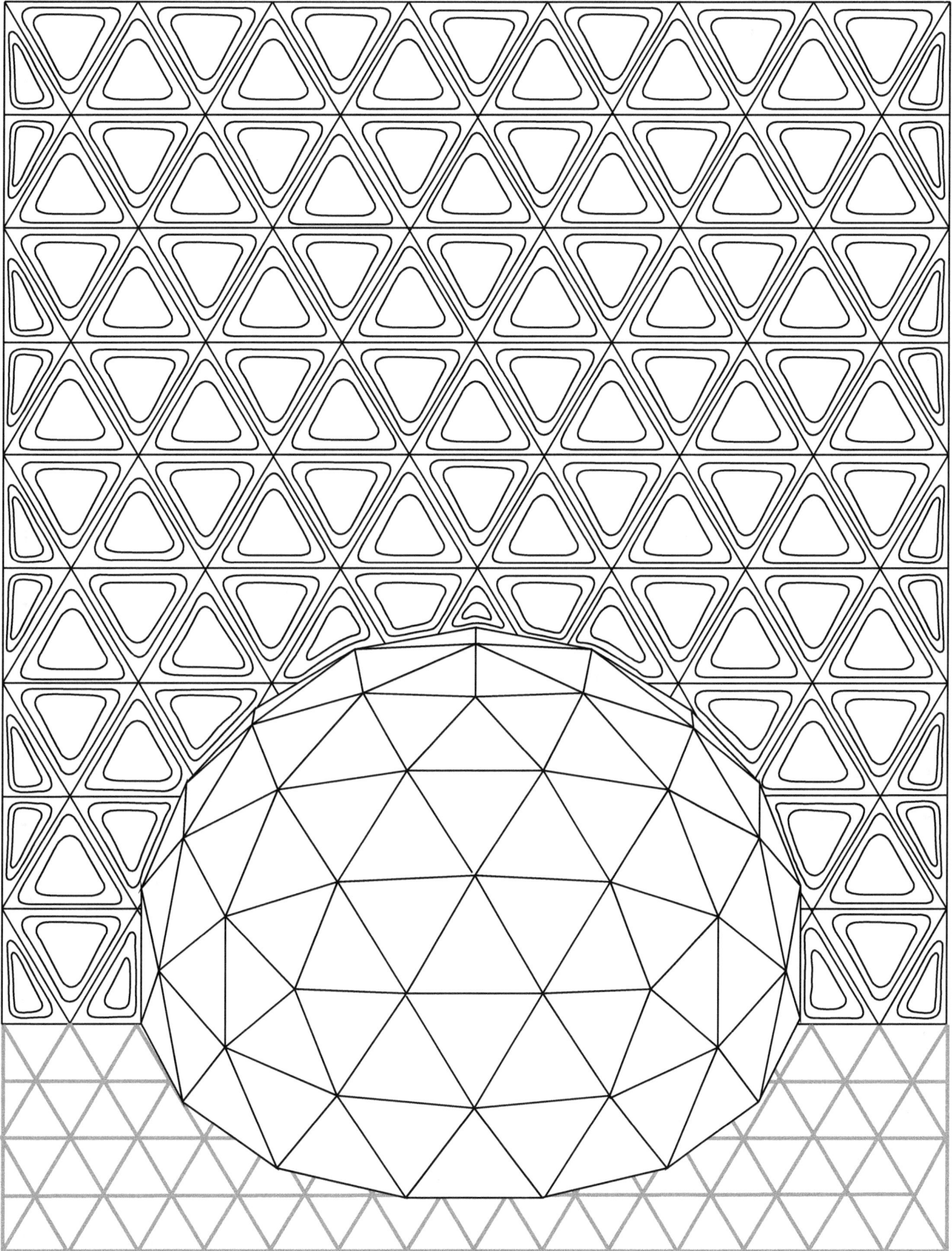

Universal Research Light Center Dome

45

Psychic Readings

47

Music! Music! Music!

Blue Ridge Mountains

© 2017 Aliyah Schick

51

SOUTHERN HIGHLANDS CRAFT GUILD

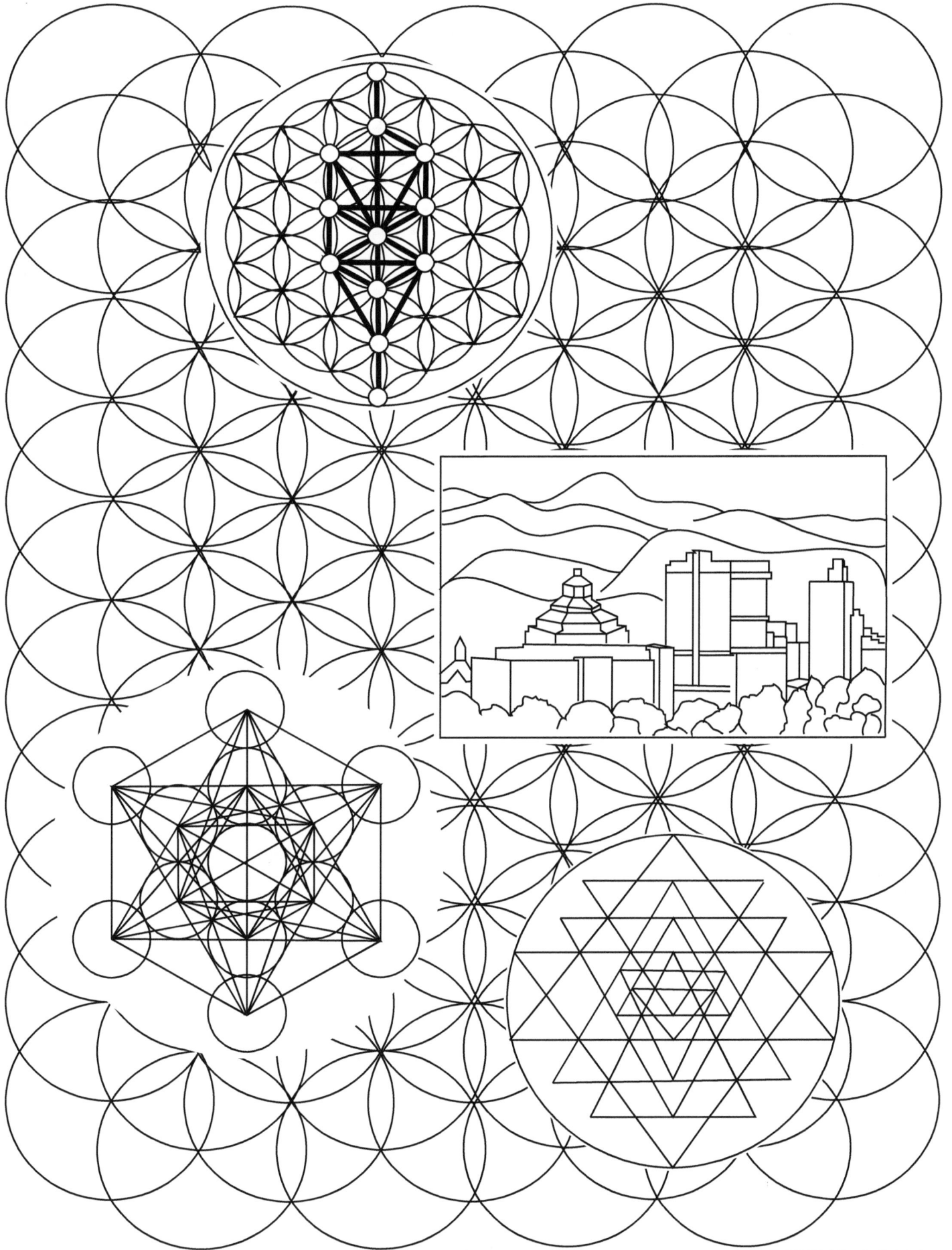

Sacred Geometry

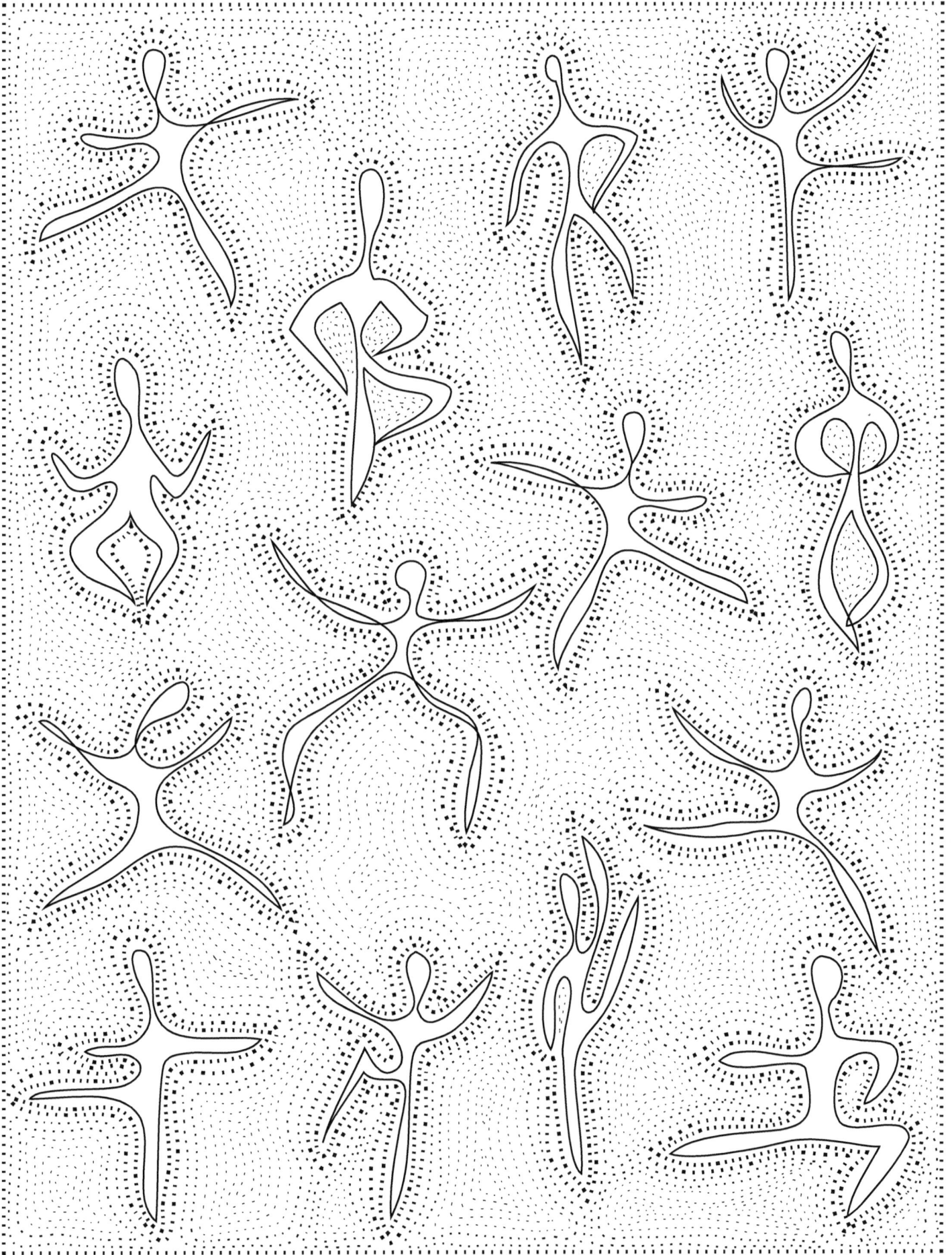

Dance!

57

Basilica of St. Lawrence

BEER CITY USA

61

OM

63

The Cherokee Nation

Prayer

Asheville City Building

Celebrate LGBTQ Diversity

3000

2900

3000

3100

3162

3000

2900

2800

2900

2900

3000

3100

3100

2900

Trail

3100

3200

3327

3100

3000

2900

3000

2900

Trail

3000

Topographical Trail Map

© 2017 Aliyah Schick

73

Fiddler

75

Biltmore

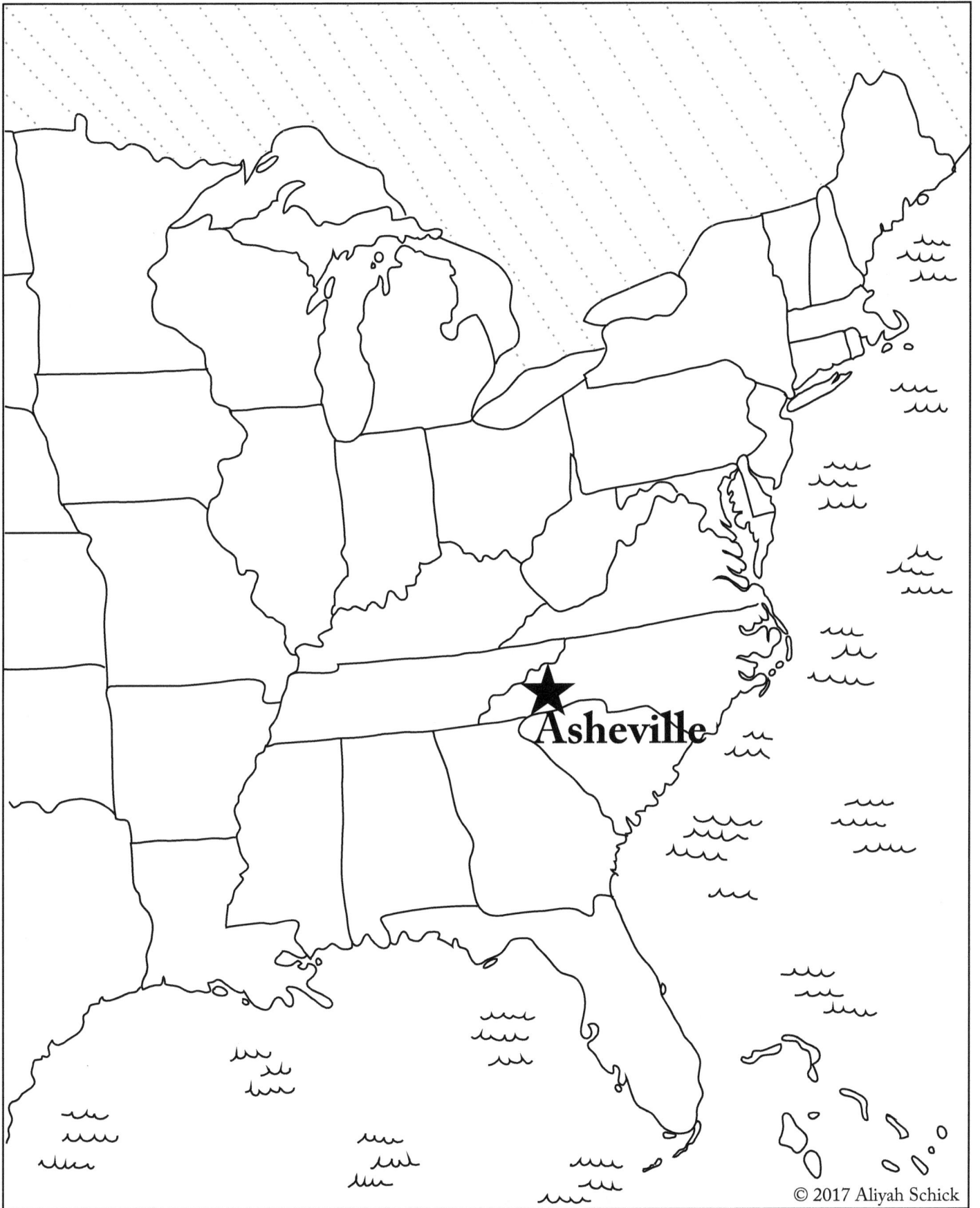

Asheville

© 2017 Aliyah Schick

You Are Here!

Kayaking

81

Fall Colors

Balanced Whole

85

One World

87

"From little acorns grow mighty oaks."

Meditation

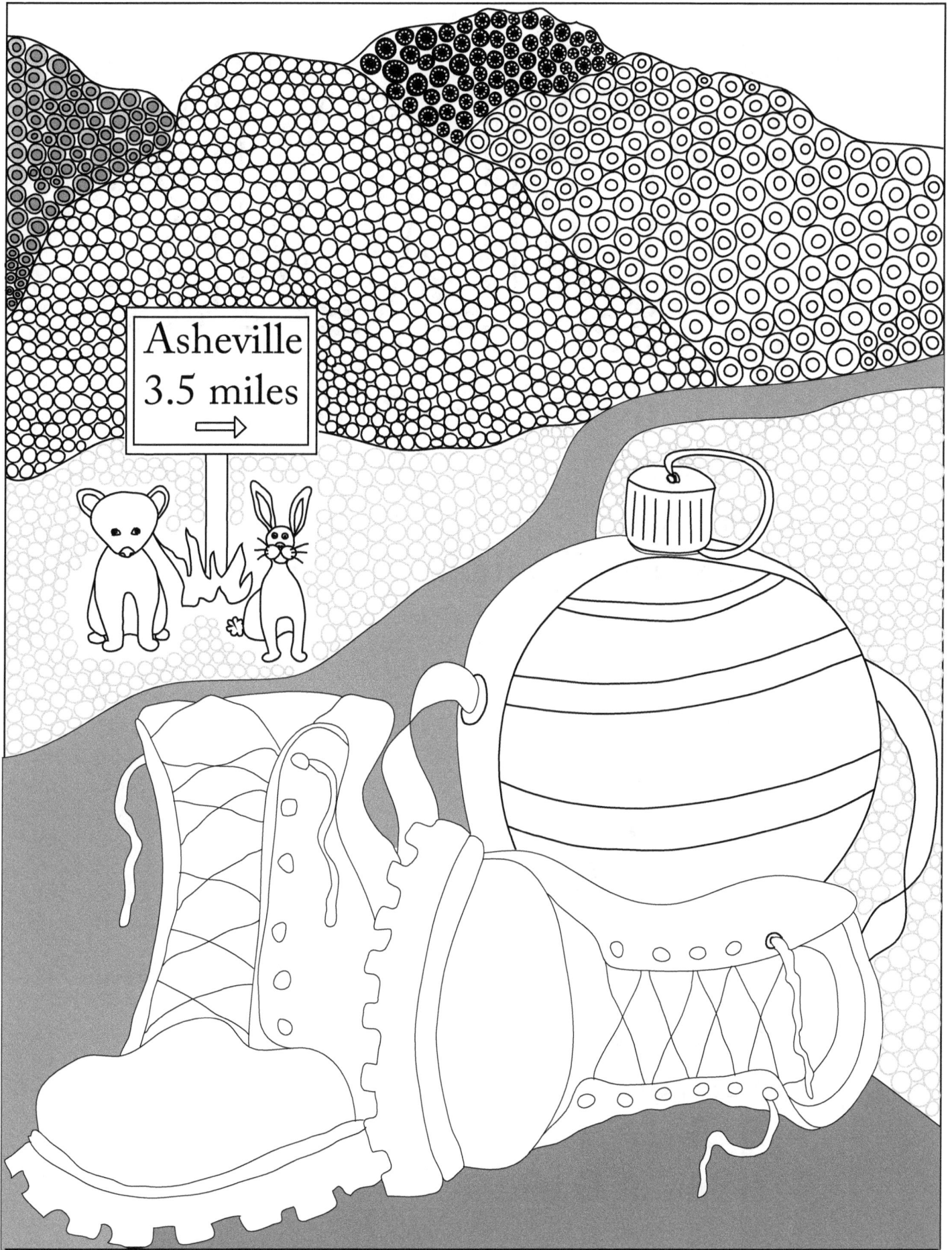

Asheville
3.5 miles
⟹

Mountains to Sea Trail

COLOR

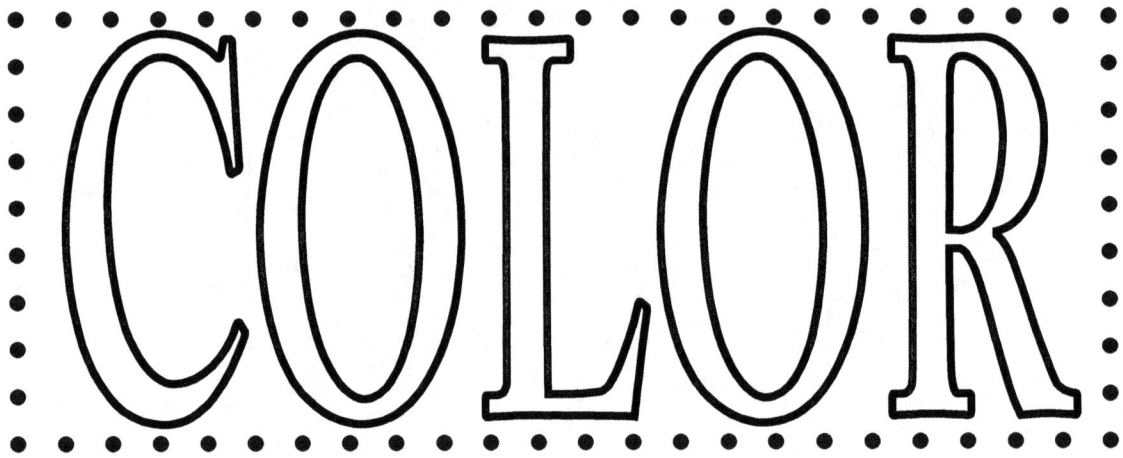

The Meditative Coloring Books Series
- **Angels**
- **Crosses**
- **Ancient Symbols**
- **Hearts**
- **Labyrinths**
- **Om**
- **Goddess**
- **Be Love**
- **Asheville**

The Jewish Coloring Books for Grown Ups
- **Judaica**
- **Alefbet**
- **Chai**
- **Star of David**

The Meditative Coloring Books Series:
Angels, Crosses, Ancient Symbols, Hearts, Labyrinths, OM, Goddess, Be Love, and Asheville

---

<u>Meditative Coloring Book 1 -- Angels</u>

These angelic images are drawn with a pen in each hand, as artist Aliyah Schick allows the lines to go where they will, mirroring each other. Every movement is guided by spirit; every drawing is different; and each one is a wonderful surprise filled with angelic presence. Immerse yourself in the angelic realm as you color these drawings. Invite the angels to come into your world, to love and support you in all you do.

<u>Meditative Coloring Book 2 -- Crosses</u>

The cross is one of the most ancient and enduring sacred symbols, found in nearly every culture from cave dwellers throughout human existence. It symbolizes the celestial, spiritual divine coming into being in this material world. It represents the sacred taking form, and the integration of soul into physical life. These 36 original artist's drawings feature ancient and contemporary images of the cross in reflections of the deep spiritual significance of its form. Let the spirit and meaning of the cross fill you as you color these images.

---

www.MeditativeColoring.com

Meditative Coloring Book 3 -- Ancient Symbols

Ancient and indigenous sacred images speak deeply to us, to our bellies and our bones, to our cellular memory and our wisdom, to our souls' yearnings. Native peoples throughout time and place see the sacred in all of life. For them, holiness is life and life is holiness. Life is the manifestation of the holy in all things. These original artist's drawings feature timeless designs used by every culture on earth to remind us of the sacred. Dip into deeply meaningful realms as you color these drawings.

Meditative Coloring Book 4 -- Hearts

The heart is one of our favorite symbols, evoking feelings of love, caring, loyalty, and devotion. As you spend time with these heart drawings, open your heart to live with more compassion for others and for yourself. Open your life to deeper connection with the earth and all of life. Open yourself to recognize the sacred in all things, including in yourself.

www.MeditativeColoring.com

Meditative Coloring Book 5 -- Labyrinths

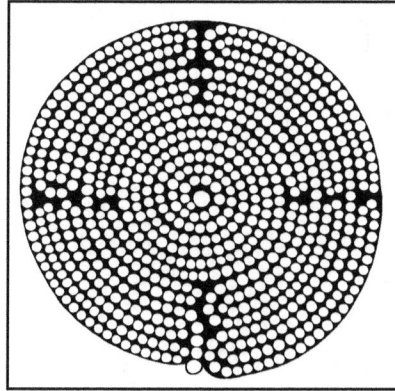

Color your steps into the labyrinth as you contemplate, meditate, or pray. Go deep into your inner wisdom and guidance where questions' answers reveal themselves and choices come clear. Or, simply relax and be with your breathing. Now you can bring your labyrinth with you to wherever you need to be. This collection of 36 original artist's drawings invites you into the labyrinth any time you wish.

Meditative Coloring Book 6 -- OM

Spend meditative time with the *OM* as you color these 36 original artist's drawings. Allow the *OM* to infuse and entune your spirit, your mind, your emotions, and every cell of your body with its pure, sacred grace. Fill yourself with its light. Become one with its beauty. Emerge relaxed, centered, calm, and at peace.

Color for relaxation, stress reduction, meditation, spiritual connection, prayer, centering, and healing. Color to calm and come into balance, to find your intuitive wisdom, and to learn to be more of your deep, true self.

www.MeditativeColoring.com

Meditative Coloring Book 7 -- Goddess

For 30,000 years in prehistoric time people all over the world celebrated and worshipped the sacred feminine. The Great Mother Goddess was the creator of all life and the life force within all life. Worship was every day here and now, holistic, visceral and sensual, all about earth, body, and nature.

Now we are seeing a revival of the sacred feminine through valuing nature, simplicity, mindfulness, meaningfulness, and clarity, along with a growing desire to honor intuition, right-brain knowing, and deep connection.

Color these 36 original artist's drawings as you open yourself to the sacred feminine in you. Nurture this long-abandoned side of conscious living, and bring yourself to a more sustainable balance.

Meditative Coloring Book 8 -- Be Love

Love starts inside yourself, with opening yourself to love. Be love to discover love. That's what this BE LOVE Meditative Coloring Book is all about. This book and its 36 original artist's drawings are designed to focus your meditative coloring on love and immerse you in the experience and sensations of loving and being loved. Coloring these pages encourages love to blossom all around and through your heart, mind, body, and spirit. Spending time in love leads to more love, which leads to more love, which leads to more love... All that love lifts up your life, and lifts up the world around you, and wow!

Meditative Coloring Book 9 -- Asheville

Come to Asheville, North Carolina, in your daydreams as you color your choice of these 36 original artist's drawings. Whether you live in Asheville, vacation here, came to summer camp here as a kid, or maybe you have yet to arrive, let go of every day life, take some deep, releasing breaths, and relax into the many delightful aspects of Asheville. Immerse yourself in the area's marvelous and varied charms -- old time fiddler, mountain scene, historic architecture, kayaker on the river, meditation, Blue Ridge Parkway, craft beer, yoga, every kind of music, faith, dance, drumming... Ground yourself into these mystical, magical mountains and feed your soul with meditative coloring in Asheville's welcoming embrace.

The Labyrinth Guided Journal, a Year in the Labyrinth

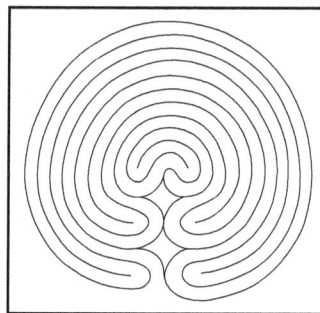

The twists and turns of the labyrinth remove you from ordinary life, and draw you deeper into willingness, into yourself, and into sacred wisdom. Use *The Labyrinth Guided Journal* on your own journey through the next year. Each week the journal offers a new thought or experience or challenge drawn from the labyrinth, and a question or suggestion for you to consider and write about throughout the week.

The Jewish Coloring Books for Grown Ups

Color for stress relaxation, Jewish meditation, Shabbat peace, and healing.

JUDAICA Coloring Book

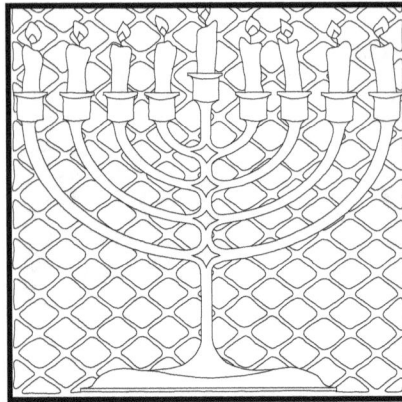

Menorah, dredel, Ten Commandment tablets, challah, Torah scrolls, Magen David, Havdalah braid, mezuzah, and more. Color these beautiful, original artist's drawings based on familiar Jewish objects and symbols. Relax, unwind, de-stress, and allow healing as you ground yourself into your Jewish heritage. L'chaim!

ALEFBET Coloring Book

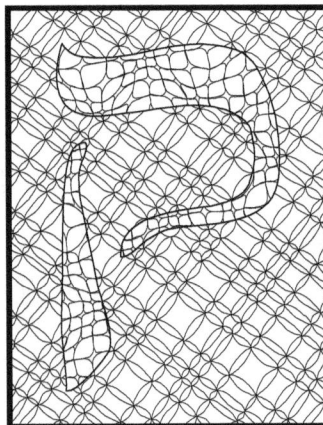

Alef, bet, gimel, dalet, hey, vav, zayin, chet, tet, yod, kaf, lamed, mem, nun, samech, ayin, peh, tsade, qof, resh, shin, and tav; 22 letters in the Hebrew alefbet. Coloring these 36 beautiful, original artist's drawings based on the Hebrew letter forms is relaxing, reduces stress, and lightens your load as it connects you with your Jewish roots. If these letters are the building blocks of the universe, then spending peaceful time coloring them can be beneficial in deeply healing ways, too.

www.JewishColoring.com

CHAI Coloring Book

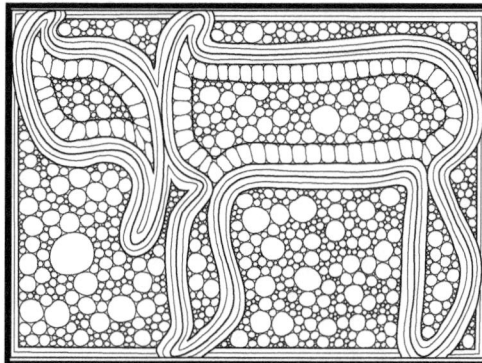

The Jewish *Chai* symbol represents the Hebrew word *chai*, meaning life. It is worn, displayed, or given as a gift as a symbol and reminder of the Jewish love for life, to celebrate being Jewish, and to bring abundant good luck. Spend relaxed, meditative time immersed in the many joys of the *Chai* as you color these 36 beautiful drawings.

STAR OF DAVID Coloring Book

The six-pointed Star of David is our most familiar Jewish symbol. Used as decoration and adornment on both religious and secular items, the Star of David represents Jewish pride in shared heritage, community, and family, and a declaration of hope and commitment. Spend time coloring these 36 original artist's drawings based on the Star of David and allow yourself to ground into your Jewish roots and celebrate your love of being Jewish.